KARATE TO WIN

J. ALLEN QUEEN

 **Sterling Publishing Co., Inc.   New York**

To my most dedicated students: Roger, David, Dyan, Mark, and Bobby.

Edited by Timothy Nolan

Photography by Samuel Jones III

Artwork by Patsy S. Queen

Queen, J. Allen.
    Karate to win / by J. Allen Queen
        p.   cm.
    Includes index.
    ISBN 0-8069-6686-6.   ISBN 0-8069-6687-4 (lib. bdg.)
    1. Karate.   I. Title.
GV1114.3.Q44   1988
796.8'153—dc19   87-36572
                                                      CIP

1   3   5   7   9   10   8   6   4   2

Copyright © 1988 by J. Allen Queen
Published by Sterling Publishing Co., Inc.
Two Park Avenue, New York, N.Y. 10016
Distributed in Canada by Oak Tree Press Ltd.
℅ Canadian Manda Group, P.O. Box 920, Station U
Toronto, Ontario, Canada M8Z 5P9
Distributed in the United Kingdom by Blandford Press
Link House, West Street, Poole, Dorset BH15 1LL, England
Distributed in Australia by Capricorn Ltd.
P.O. Box 665, Lane Cove, NSW 2066
Manufactured in the United States of America
All rights reserved
Sterling ISBN 0-8069-6686-6 Trade
                6687-4 Library

CONTENTS

Acknowledgments

I would like to thank the following students for their assistance: Israel Angeles, Jordan Angeles, Antwaine Brown, Dyan Byers, Jonathan Jones, Bobby Knott, Jonathan Lovelace, Heather McDowell, Scott Myers, Alex Queen, Travis Queen, Heather Roberts, Brad Splawn, Max Washington, Travis Watson, Joey Whitaker, Renada Wingo, Robert Wingo, Jr., and Robert Wingo III.

1
WINNING IN KARATE

Winning! Do you like to win? Then you have chosen the right book. Here, you will learn the basic skills of karate, including blocking, striking, kicking, and punching.

Illus. 1. By learning these skills, you can be a winner in karate, receive trophies, and be recognized as a winner by your friends.

But first, you need to understand the formula for winning. It includes three things:

1. Positive Attitude

Illus. 2. Be positive about school and home.

Look at your karate practice as an improvement in your life. Develop strong values. Avoid things that will hurt you.

2. Mental Discipline

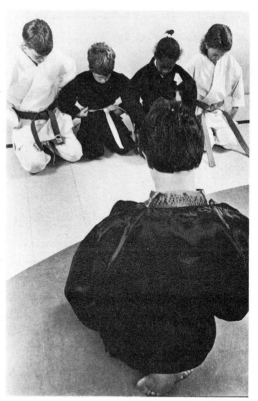

Illus. 3. How you think controls your physical skills.

Mental discipline will give you the control to be a winner. You will improve your concentration, thus improving your karate skills. You will be more dedicated to mastering each skill. You will also control your anger better.

3. Physical Fitness

Illus. 4. Physical fitness is very important in karate.

By practising the exercises starting on page 21, you will improve the karate skills you will learn in this book to be a winner.

POSITIVE ATTITUDE + MENTAL DISCIPLINE + PHYSICAL FITNESS = WINNING

Now that you have the formula for winning, you need some background information about karate competition.

Karate Competitions

Every year thousands of tournaments are held throughout the world for students, like you, who are studying karate. You enter by age, size, and ability level or rank.

You can enter a *kata* (ka-tuh) competition, where you demonstrate a prearranged set of kicks, punches, and blocks that show your karate ability. Kata is something like a dance.

Illus. 5. In kata, you face the judges, ask permission to perform, and then do your kata.

All katas have names. Some katas have such names as "The Breathing Dragon" or "Crane on a Rock." Some have Japanese names, such as *Heian*. There are hundreds of katas. You'll learn kata on page 97.

Illus. 6. After you perform your kata, you receive a score from each judge. The highest total score wins. Awards are given for first, second, and third place.

You can also compete in freestyle sparring. This is called *kumite* (koo-ma-ta). In kumite, it's important not to fear your opponent, but respect his ability and skill as you respect your own. Your goal is to score a kick or punch to the head or body without being blocked.

Illus. 7. In kumite you spar an opponent.

You may face several types of opponents.

Illus. 8 (left). Some kumite fighters are tall and lean . . .

Illus. 9 (right). . . . others short and fast.

12

Illus. 10. Some fighters are considered "bulls" and hard to move.

Illus. 11. Others are "bouncers," who move around the ring.

Illus. 12. A "charger" is very aggressive, throwing many punches and kicks quickly.

Illus. 13. Still others are defensive fighters, who block kicks and punches from their opponents and strike while being attacked.

Karate tournaments also offer self-defense demonstrations and musical and weapons kata. In this book, you will focus on kata and kumite.

One warning—karate was designed as a martial art, or fighting art, but it is not only for fighting or self-defense. For the great masters, karate is a way of life. *The last thing* you ever want to do is hurt someone, unless an attacker is endangering your life.

Karate was developed in the Orient, and is now popular all over the world. For the past thirty years, sport karate has been a major hobby for thousands of students. In karate, you combine kicks, punches, and strikes for self-defense, kumite, or kata. Although many students follow a strong disciplined approach, some students prefer only the physical aspects of karate. These students do not truly know karate and are not winners.

Illus. 14. There are usually three judges for a kumite match, and there is always great respect between the judges and the fighters. You will learn kumite on page 65.

2

GETTING READY FOR COMPETITION

Although any loose pants and a sweat shirt are fine for practice sessions, you will need a *gi* (gee), or karate suit, to enter a tournament. Karate suits come in a variety of sizes, colors, and styles.

Illus. 17 (below). As you progress in karate, you may like a more colorful or flashy suit. These suits are made of satinlike material, but they're much stronger.

Illus. 15 (above). The traditional suit is the most common. It usually comes in either white or black.

Illus. 16 (above, right). Some students choose to mix colors. You can add colored stripes to the suit. Some students like to add a patch, representing their karate club or organization.

Illus. 18 (left). If your mother has offered to sew your karate suit, patterns, as well as suits, can be ordered from companies advertised in karate magazines.

Illus. 19 (right). Suits come in sizes from zero for infants and toddlers (although you will not see many very young children in karate) through size seven, which is for people over six feet tall.

One additional item is needed to make your karate suit complete: the belt. As a beginner, you will wear a white belt. When you improve your skills over the next few years, your rank will increase to yellow, orange, green, blue, brown, and then black. Generally, the darker the belt, the higher the rank. With few exceptions, you will be matched with students of the same rank when you enter a tournament.

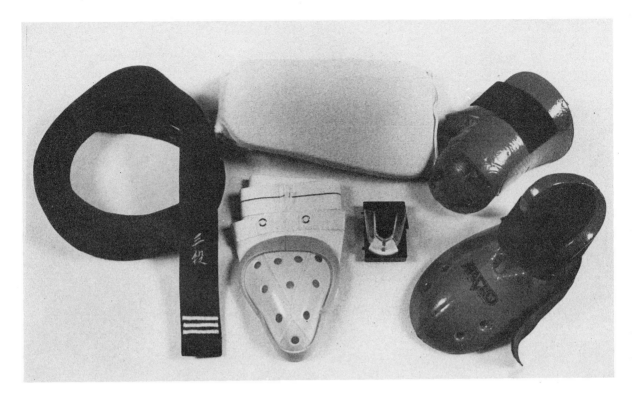

Illus. 20. In addition to the belt (*far left*), you will need hand and foot gloves (*far right*) and a mouth guard (*center*). Boys should also wear an athletic supporter (*center left*).

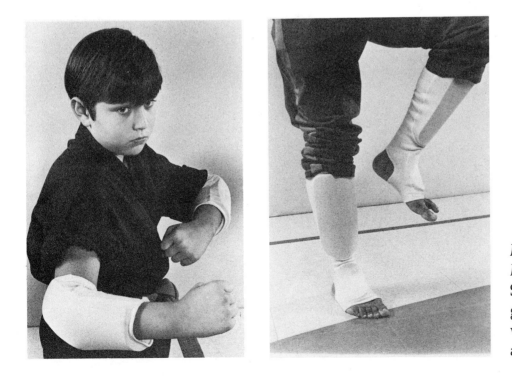

Illus. 21 (left) and Illus. 22 (right). Some boys and girls also like to wear shin pads and elbow pads.

19

Although you can learn the basic skills of karate from this book, you will have to join a karate school and be evaluated by a sensei *(sen say)*, or teacher, before you can receive a belt. You will also need to study under a qualified instructor before you can learn and master advanced karate skills. One karate organization, just for kids, is the International Children's Karate Association, known as ICKA *(e kuh)*. Located in Raleigh, North Carolina, this organization can refer you to qualified instructors in your area. In addition, ICKA can provide you with information concerning karate tournaments, equipment, and information just for children in karate.

3
EXERCISES FOR WINNING

Exercise is an important part of karate. It is necessary to warm up your muscles before a karate workout, and it will help you improve your karate skills. The three elements you want to work for are balance, flexibility, and speed.

These exercises should be done in order. Begin them slowly. Before long you will notice that you have better balance, and you will be able to stretch further as your muscles become more flexible. Speed will improve with practice.

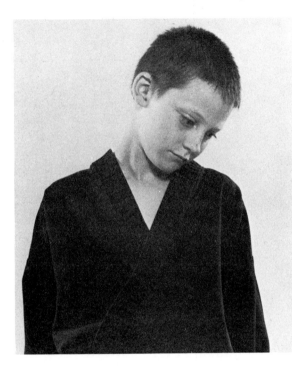

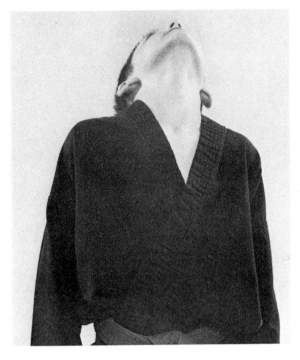

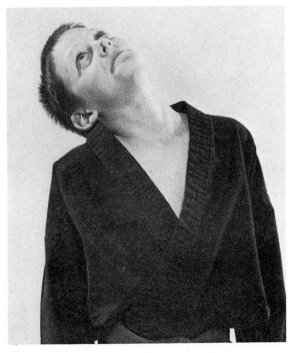

Neck Roll

Begin with your head held straight.

Illus. 23 (above, left). Roll your neck to the left, then towards the back.

Illus. 24 (above). Now push your neck far back and then to the right.

Illus. 25 (left). Finish by returning your head to the beginning position. Repeat five times and then rotate from the right five times.

Arm Rotation

The arm rotation will loosen your shoulders, neck, and arms.

Illus. 26 (above, left). Stand straight with your right arm down by your side. Slowly lift your right arm upwards and close to your head.

Illus. 27 (above). At this point swing your right arm behind you.

Illus. 28 (left). Finish by returning it to the original position. Do this five times and then do the same exercise with your left arm.

Toe Stand

This exercise will strengthen your legs and help you balance better.

Illus. 29 (right). Stand straight with your arms at your side.

Illus. 30 (left). Lift your arms straight in the air and stand on your toes. Return to the original position and repeat five times.

25

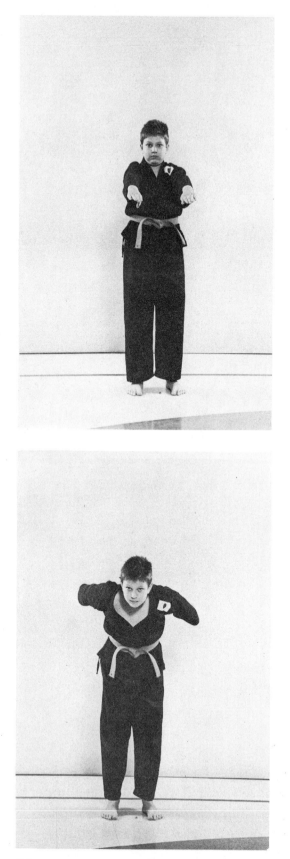

Back Stretch

In this exercise you will loosen up muscles in your back and shoulders.

Illus. 31 (above, left). Stand erect and extend your arms straight out in front of you.

Illus. 32 (above). Now stretch your arms upwards as high as possible.

Illus. 33 (left). Next, bend your body to the front and lift your arms backwards as high as possible.

Balance Walk

Illus. 34 (left). In the balance walk, you stand with your right foot directly in front of your left.

Illus. 35 (right). Take a step forward, placing your left foot in front. Keep your arms extended straight out. Imagine you are walking on a tightrope and take 15–20 steps.

Toe Lifts

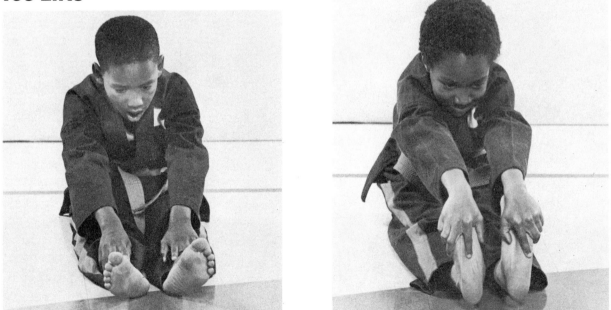

Illus. 36 (left). Sit on the floor and bend forward with your legs extended straight out.
Illus. 37 (right). Grasp your toes and lift your heels off the ground. Hold for 2 seconds. Repeat five times.

Body Bends

Body bends will increase your flexibility.

Illus. 38 (left). Stand straight, with your feet a shoulders' width apart and your hands touching.

Illus. 40 (above). Now bring your feet closer together while you stand.

Illus. 39 (left). Without bending your knees, move downwards and reach as close to the floor as possible. *Caution:* Do these slowly and don't force *too hard.* With time and practice, you will easily reach the floor. After touching the floor, return to the original position. Do this exercise five times.

Illus. 41 (above). Repeat the same move downward five times.

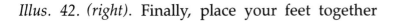

Illus. 42. (right). Finally, place your feet together

Illus. 43. (right). Touch the floor. Remember, do not bend your knees.

Leg Lifts

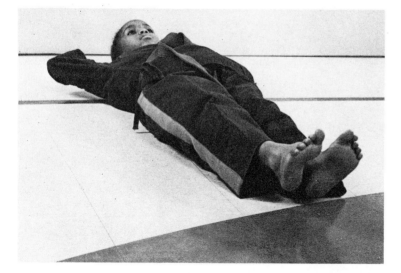

Leg lifts will help strengthen your stomach and leg muscles.

Illus. 44 (left). Place your hand behind your head and put your feet together on the floor.

Illus. 45 (right). Lift your legs 6 inches off the floor and hold for 10 seconds. Drop your feet to the floor. Repeat and hold your feet off the floor for 15 seconds, then 20, etc.

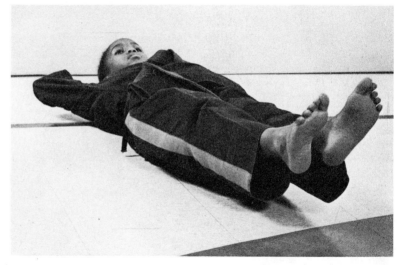

Illus. 46 (below). When you reach 30 seconds holding your feet off the floor, spread your legs and lift for 10, 20, and then 30 seconds. In time you may be able to do this for 2 minutes or more.

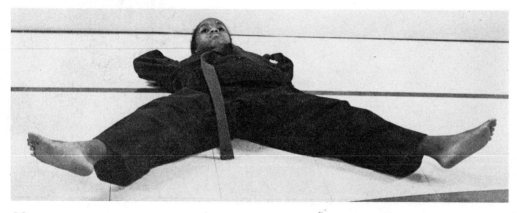

Split

Splits help make you more flexible. They also help you kick higher and faster.

Illus. 47 (left). Stand with your legs spread a shoulders' width apart.

Illus. 48 (right). Turn your right foot to the right.

Illus. 49 (right). Slowly spread your legs and stretch your body to the floor.

Illus. 50 (left). Drop your hands to the floor on both sides of your right leg and continue to push towards the floor. *Be careful.* Try to stretch farther each day. But don't push if it becomes painful.

Illus. 51 (right). In time, you will be able to move your legs into a full side split.

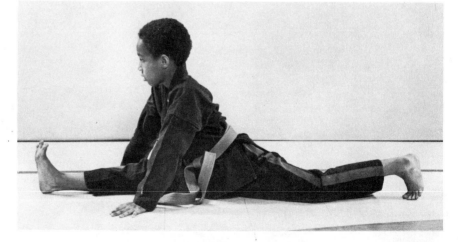

Leg Stretch

Illus. 52 (right). Sit with your legs wide apart.

Illus. 53 (left). Bend forward and grab your right ankle.

Illus. 54 (right). Repeat five times. Do the same exercise to the left. Repeat five times.

Partner Exercises

Illus. 55 (right). Have a partner lift your leg upwards as you direct him. Do it with your left leg and right leg. Start slowly and increase your height with time.

Illus. 56 (left). Sit directly in front of your partner. He grabs your arms and places his feet inside of your knees. *Slowly and carefully* he pulls you to him.

Illus. 57 (right). Now stand in front of your partner. Place your hands (palms upwards) under his hands (palms downwards).

Illus. 58 (left). Now, quickly, move your right or left hand to tap his face lightly without being blocked. Reverse hands, and you try to block.

Illus. 59 (right). Place your right hand out in front of your partner.

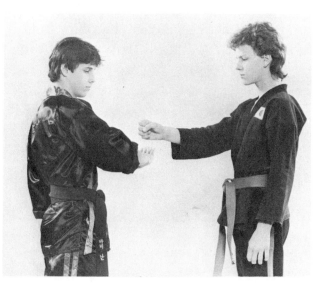

Illus. 60 (left). As he moves to grab, quickly move to the side. Avoid getting caught.

As you increase your speed, try this exercise:

Illus. 61 (left). Face your partner with your right foot next to his right foot and your right hand next to his right hand.

Illus. 62 (right). Quickly, drop your hand and try to touch his face. Remember he is trying to do the same. This is an excellent exercise to do before kumite. The goal is the tap (light touch). DO NOT SLAP!

You should do these exercises as a warm-up to your karate practice. It is easy to hurt a muscle by not warming up properly. Take your time. Work hard. You will see progress soon.

4
WINNING KARATE SKILLS

You are now ready to learn karate. In this section, you will learn the basic techniques: stances, blocks, punches, strikes, and kicks. These techniques are the ones most often used in kumite and kata competition.

STANCES

The stance is the most important part of karate. It must be strong to support your weight. Keep your back straight, and face in the direction of the stance. The major stances (front and side views) are shown in the photographs. The foot positions are shown in the drawings.

Closed Stance

Use the closed stance when you bow to your instructor or opponent. Place your weight equally on both feet and keep them close together.

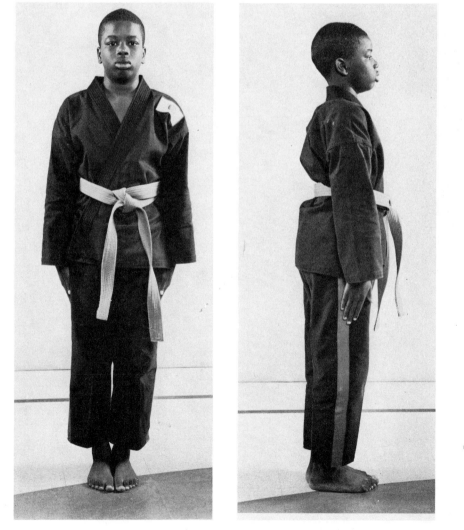

Illus. 63. Front view.   *Illus. 64.* Side view.   *Illus. 65.* Foot position.

Open Stance

Also known as the ready or set stance, the open stance is used at the beginning and end of most karate exercises. Place your weight equally on both feet. Your feet should be a shoulders' width apart.

Illus.66. Front view.

Illus. 67. Side view.

Illus. 68. Foot position.

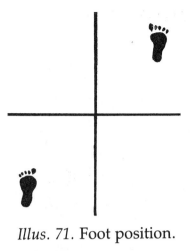

Illus. 71. Foot position.

Illus. 69. Front view.

Illus. 70. Side view.

Front Stance

Perhaps the most frequently used stance, the front stance allows you to move to the front or to the rear. Keep your back leg straight and your knee locked. In the right stance, place your right leg in front. Bend your right leg at the knee and keep a little more than half of your weight on it. Do the opposite for the left front stance.

Back Stance

Illus. 72. Front view.

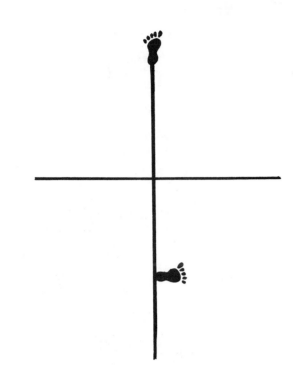

Illus. 74. Foot position.

Illus. 73. Side view.

Another useful stance is the back stance. In the right back stance put three-quarters of your body weight on your right leg. Bend both knees, but bend your right knee more deeply than the left knee. The heels of both your feet should be in a straight line.

42

Cat Stance

In this stance you will look like a cat crouching and ready to strike. Put most of your body weight on your right leg so that your left leg just touches the floor. You shift all your weight to the right leg in the right cat stance when you kick with your left leg. For the left cat stance, place your left leg behind and place your right leg in front.

Illus. 77. Foot position.

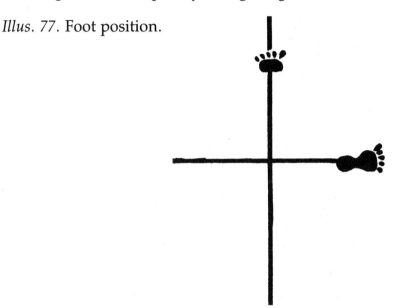

Illus. 76. Side view.

Illus. 75. Front view.

Illus. 78. Front view.

Illus. 79. Side view.

Illus. 80. Foot position.

Horse Stance

Pretend you are riding a horse as you practise the horse stance. With your feet two shoulders' widths apart, bend both knees deeply. Keep your back straight. You may find this stance difficult in the beginning, but with practice it will become easier. In the horse stance, you can use several different strikes and blocks. Many karate students use the horse stance when sparring.

BLOCKS

You will use blocks for defense to prevent an opponent's punch or kick from hitting you.

Rising Block

Use the rising block to stop a downward blow to the head.

Illus. 81 (left). Get into a left front stance to do a left rising block, with your left hand in front. Bring your left arm across your chest, palm downward. Your right fist is at your right hip.

Illus. 82 (right). Turn your left arm so that your palm faces upwards and drive your left arm up to meet the strike. Do the opposite for a right rising block.

Outside Middle Block

You can protect your middle and upper body with the outside middle block.

Illus. 83 (right). From a left front stance, push your right hand forward as you pull your left hand back near your head.

Illus. 84 (left). With a swift turn of your body to the right, drive your left arm completely across your body. At the same time, pull your right arm back to your right hip. Do the opposite for a right outside middle block.

Inside Middle Block

Use the inside middle block to protect your upper body.

Illus. 85 (left). In a left front stance, place your left arm across your chest while placing the right arm on the right hip.

Illus. 86 (right). Like a coiled spring, snap the left arm upwards to block. Do the opposite for a right inside block.

Low Block

Use a low block to block the lower body area.

Illus. 87 (above). From a left front stance place your left arm across your body with the hand near the right side of the head. Keep the right arm resting on the right hip.

Illus. 88 (above, right). To block, drive the left hand straight downwards.

Illus. 89 (right). As you block, the left arm is out in front and your right hand remains on your right hip ready to punch.

Cross Block

Known as a cross block or "X" block, this can block a strike downwards to the head or a kick to the groin.

Illus. 90 (above, left). Get in a horse stance and cross both arms at the chest.

Illus. 91 (above). Quickly drive both arms downwards, still crossed, to block a kick.

Illus. 92 (left). Return the hands to the chest and drive upwards and crossed to block a downwards strike or hammer blow.

PUNCHES AND STRIKES

Forward Punch

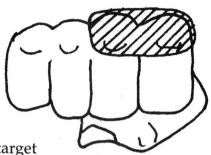

Illus. 93 (right). Close your fists tightly and strike the target with the first two knuckles to do the front punch.

Illus. 94. Stand in a horse stance with both hands by your side. Fists are held upside down.

Illus. 95. Take your right hand and push out while turning your wrist with knuckles upwards. Extend into a full punch.

Illus. 96 (right). Now push your left hand out while turning the wrist. At the same time pull back your right wrist.

Illus. 97 (left). Extend the left hand to full punch. The right hand should now rest upside down on your right hip.

Reverse Punch

Perhaps the most used punch in ku-mite today is the reverse punch. It is fast and can be very accurate.

Illus. 98 (right). Stand in either a back, front, or horse stance. Use your left hand to cover your body in case of an attack. Pull your right hand tightly by your side. Turn your body slightly.

Illus. 99 (left). Push the right hand outward while turning the fist up-wards.

Illus. 100 (left). Extend fully, striking the target with the punch.

Illus. 101 (right). Immediately, upon contact, snap the hand back to your chest and move the right hand back into the original position. Use this technique to strike an opponent as he is charging with an attack. This is known as "beating the man to the punch," since he began the attack and you blocked and struck the opponent.

Knife-Hand Punch

Illus. 102 (right). With your left hand in front for protection, pull the right, with fingers fully extended, behind the right side of the head.

Illus. 103 (below). With a driving twist, turn your body to the left and begin to extend the knife-hand outward.

Illus. 104 (below, right). Continue until the hand is fully extended and the target is struck.

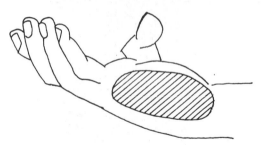

Illus. 105 (left). Known as the "karate chop," the knife-hand uses the outer edge of your hand.

Back Fist

Illus. 106 (left). Stand in a horse stance with your right arm held parallel to the floor in front of your chest. Your left fist remains at your hip.

Illus. 107 (below, left). As fast as possible, snap your arm directly out to the side, striking the target with the knuckles of your index finger and middle finger.

Illus. 108 (below). Pull your fist back quickly, and return it to the front of your chest.

Illus. 109 (above). Strike with the shaded area.

Ridge Hand

Use the ridge hand to strike to the head.

Illus. 110 (above, left). With your left hand in front for protection, swing your right arm and hand as far behind you as possible.

Illus. 111 (above). As you begin to strike, swing the arm with the elbow extended as you turn your body to the target.

Illus. 112 (left). Extend the arm fully to strike the target.

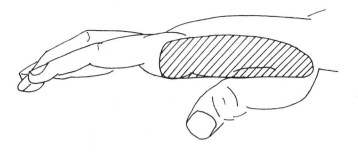

Illus. 113 (left). The inside edge of the hand is the striking area. Be sure to pull your thumbs under the striking area.

KICKS

Your leg muscles are larger and therefore stronger than your arm muscles. You will discover that your kicks are the strongest weapons available to your body. It is important to realize, however, that your kicks will be slower and less accurate than your punches. But with time your accuracy and speed will improve greatly. You will find that balancing while kicking will be difficult. You must learn to shift your weight to one leg when you kick. This will improve with dedicated practice.

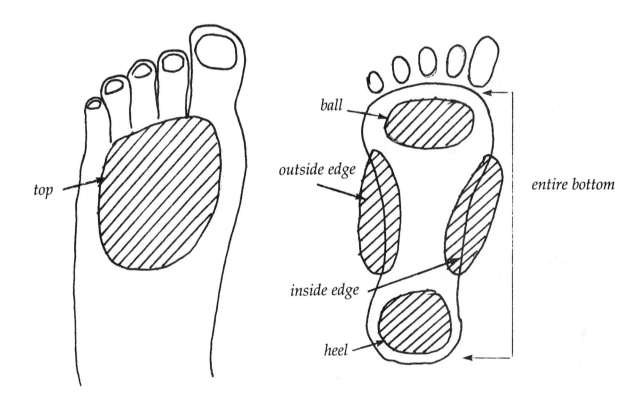

Illus. 114 (left) and Illus. 115 (right). The foot has six major areas that are used for striking: the top, ball, heel, inside edge, outside edge, and the entire bottom.

Front Snap Kick

Use a snapping action of the knee to deliver an effective front kick.

Illus. 116 (right). To do a right front snap kick stand in a left front stance. Raise your right knee to waist level. Pull back with your right foot and raise your toes for the kick.

Illus. 117 (below). Snap your right leg forward and deliver the kick, striking with the ball of your foot.

Illus. 118 (below, right). Use a whipping action and snap your kick back to a holding position. Set your foot back into a left front stance. Do the opposite for a left front kick.

Power Side Kick

You can use a power side kick to strike an opponent's head, chest, or stomach. Start low and as your flexibility increases so will the heights of your kicks.

Illus. 119 (left). Stand in a horse stance. Lift your right leg so that your foot is at your left knee.

Illus. 120 (below, left). Turn your body to the left and extend your leg straight out, striking the target with the outer edge of your foot.

Illus. 121 (below). Snap the leg back. Return your foot to the left knee. Return to a horse stance. Do the opposite for a left side kick.

Roundhouse Kick

The roundhouse is a powerful kick which can be thrown at lightning speed. Round-house kicks can be delivered to the head, chest, stomach and groin.

Illus. 122 (opposite page, top left). As with the side kick, begin the kick low, from a right back stance. Raise your right foot behind your right hip. You must balance on your left leg.

Illus. 123 (opposite page, top right). Turn your body and raise your knee.

Illus. 124 (opposite page, bottom left). Drop your body back as you raise your leg higher in a striking position.

Illus. 125 (opposite page, bottom right). Snap your right leg and strike the target with the ball of your foot.

Illus. 126 (below, left). Immediately snap your leg back. Continue to lower the foot after the kick.

Illus. 127 (below, right). Return to a back stance. Do the opposite for the left leg.

Spinning Back Kick

Use the spinning back kick to strike an opponent to the head, chest, or stomach. This kick is usually used when an opponent is "faked out" or caught off guard. Always keep your eye on the target.

Illus. 128 (left). Stand in a ready stance or horse stance and lift your right leg as high as possible.

Illus. 129 (below, left). Spin your body to the right as you rotate your weight on your left foot.

Illus. 130 (below). Push your head forward and extend your right leg directly behind you, striking the target with the bottom of your foot. Do the opposite to spin kick with the left leg.

Front Thrust Kick

The front thrust kick is more power-ful than the snap kick. It also has a greater reach to strike your target. It differs only from the snap kick in that the heel of the foot is the strik-ing area.

Illus. 131 (right). Stand in a left front stance.

Illus. 132 (below). Lift your right leg to your left knee.

Illus. 133 (below, right). Pull your body backwards and drive the kick to the target.

Illus. 134. Return the kick immediately to the left knee. Place your right leg back into the original position. Do the opposite for a left front thrust kick.

5
WINNING KUMITE

Kumite, or freestyle sparring, is the most exciting part of tournament competition. Since you have no idea of what your opponent will do, you must be prepared for any kick or punch. Your opponent is a moving target. Both of you will be trying to score points with kicks, punches, and strikes. Timing and being in the best position are two of the most important things to learn in order to score and win the match.

Illus. 135 (left). When you arrive at a tournament, you will be assigned a number. Most tournaments open with an official bow to signal the beginning of the competition.

Illus. 136 (right). Numerous trophies are awarded in several divisions, as determined by age, size, and rank.

BEGINNING THE MATCH

Illus. 137. When a match begins you and your opponent will face the middle judge and give a respectful bow.

Illus. 138. You then bow to each other. There will be at least two other judges calling the match.

Illus. 139. After the official bow, place yourself in a fighting position, such as a front, back, or horse stance. The middle judge then begins the match.

POINTS

Illus. 140 (left). Points are awarded when a kick, punch, or strike to a vulnerable area of the body such as the head, chest, stomach, ribs, or neck is not blocked.

Illus. 141 (above). Watch for the middle judge to call for a point. The judges award points by raising one hand and pointing to the student who scored. There must be a majority vote—two of the three judges must agree upon the point.

Illus. 142 (right). When there is no point, the judges cross their arms downwards.

Illus. 143 (right). You punch at your opponent and it is blocked.

Illus. 144 (left). The judge awards no point.

Illus. 145 (right). This time you are not blocked.

Illus. 146 (left). You are awarded a point.

Illus. 147 (right). Sometimes you deliver a punch or kick and it is not blocked. You and your opponent are in a position where one or two judges may not see the point.

Illus. 148 (left). The judge did not see the point and signals as shown here. Tournament rules vary, but in some situations, if one judge sees a point and the other two do not disagree but simply did not see—a point may be awarded.

INFRACTIONS

Illus. 149. If you see a judge raise his hand with a circular motion, the match is stopped.

Illus. 150. If the judge then places his hand in front of his face vertically, an infraction has occurred.

When you kick too low, use an outside sweep or inside sweep, or make too much contact, you can receive an infraction. You can also receive an infraction if you are disrespectful to the judge, lose your temper, move out of the ring, or delay the match. If you punch after a judge calls a halt to the match, that is also an infraction.

If you commit an infraction, the judges can either give a warning, award a point to your opponent, or disqualify you. Again, rules vary from tournament to tournament.

THE KUMITE MATCH

The match usually lasts for 2 minutes. If you score the first three points, you are the winner. If no opponent has 3 points at the end of the match, the one with the most points wins. If neither you nor your opponent have any points, or there is a tie, the match continues until the first point is scored. If you score the point, you will be the winner.

The end of the match is similar to the beginning.

Illus. 151 (right). You and your opponent bow to the middle judge to show respect.

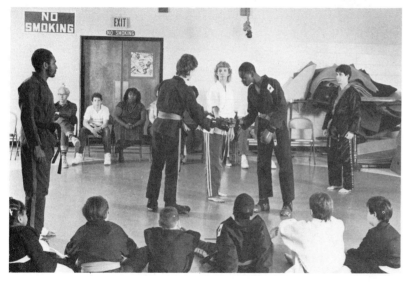

Illus. 152 (left). Then you bow to your opponent and you shake hands.

Illus. 153 (right). The middle judge declares you the winner by raising your hand. If it is the final match, you are awarded a trophy.

HURTING YOUR OPPONENT

If you accidentally hit your opponent and he is hurt, the appropriate action is to sit in a meditation position or on your knees with your back to your opponent while he or she is helped. You probably will be disqualified for excessive contact.

Illus. 154. Always try to avoid this situation.

Kumite in the lower belts should be done without actually hitting your opponent. The objective is to stop your kick or punch one inch from the opponent's body. However, rules are changing. In many tournaments light contact to the body is required. *Control your kicks and punches.* Karate is an art. It was only intended to cause pain in the event self-defense is required to protect you from an attack.

OFFENSIVE TECHNIQUES

You will begin by practising scoring techniques from an offensive approach.

Illus. 155. Get into a fighting stance (cat, horse, or front) and hold your hands high to guard your body and head.

Illus. 156 (left). With lightning speed, cross over the opponent's block and strike with a left back fist.

Situation 2:

Illus. 157 (right). Close in on your opponent and deliver a front punch to the stomach.

Illus. 158 (right). Charge your opponent, protecting yourself with your left hand.

Illus. 159 (left). Jump and throw a reverse punch to the head of the opponent.

Illus. 160 (left). Guard your opponent's front hand.

Illus. 161 (right). Deliver a front punch to the head.

Situation 5:

Illus. 162 (right). From a left front stance, fake a front kick to your opponent's stomach.

Illus. 163 (left). Just before you complete the kick, twist your right leg so that it is parallel with the floor.

Illus. 164 (left). Continue turning, keeping your knee high, and begin to extend your leg into a right roundhouse kick.

Illus. 165 (right). Complete the kick by fully extending the legs and scoring with the roundhouse to the head. Return your leg to the original position. Once you master the kick, it is very difficult to block.

Situation 6:

Illus. 166 (right). From a front or back stance throw a front kick to your opponent's stomach.

Illus. 167 (left). This same kick can be thrown to the head area.

Illus. 168 (left). In a horse stance or cat stance, pull in your right leg.

Illus. 169 (right). Deliver a side kick to the opponent's chest or stomach. Be careful and watch your control.

While sparring offensively, watch for open areas to the head and body of your opponent. Use the above seven situations, but experiment using many combinations of kicks and punches. Use variety on your offense, such as changing from a front stance to a horse stance. Throw combinations of front, side and roundhouse kicks followed by front punches, back fists or knife hand strikes.

DEFENSIVE TECHNIQUES

Illus. 170. Many students prefer to fight defensively. They like to block an opponent's advance and score with a countermove.

Situation 8:

Illus. 171. Your opponent throws a punch to your head. You block with a middle block.

Illus. 172 (left). Counter with a front kick to the stomach.

Situation 9:

Illus. 173. In this situation, your opponent attempts a punch. Block with your left hand and deliver a ridge hand to the head of your opponent.

Situation 10:

Illus. 174. Block your opponent's back fist.

Illus. 175. Counter with a punch to the head.

Situation 11:

Illus. 176. In this attack, your opponent attempts to score with a punch to the head. Use either a middle block or rising block to deflect the punch.

Illus. 177. Immediately strike with a reverse punch to the stomach or side.

Situation 12:

Illus. 178. Block your opponent's back fist.

Illus. 179. Strike with a knife hand to the neck.

Situation 13:

Illus. 180. In this situation, your opponent charges in with a jumping forward punch. Lower your body and block with a rising upper block.

Illus. 181. Score with a reverse punch with your right hand to the body.

Situation 14:

Illus. 182 (right). Your opponent delivers a front kick to your body. Block the kick with a lower block.

Illus. 183. This turns your opponent around where you can score with a punch.

Illus. 184. Use either a punch to the body or to the head.

Illus. 185 (left). Block your opponent's front kick with a left lower block.

Illus. 186 (right). Set your hand for a left back fist.

Illus. 187 (right). Quickly strike with the back fist to the head for the score.

Situation 16:

Illus. 188 (right). In this situation, your opponent delivers a front right lunging punch to your head.

Illus. 189 (left). You block with a right middle block.

Illus. 190 (right). Score with a left punch to the head.

SCORING SECRETS

Here are some other combinations you can use to score against your opponent:

Illus. 191 (right). Throw a front kick to your opponent's lower stomach area.

Illus. 192 (below). Immediately follow with a punch to the head...

Illus. 193 (below, right)... or to the chest.

You can also use fakes to draw your opponent off guard.

Illus. 194 (left). Pretend you are throwing a back fist to your opponent's head.

Illus. 195 (right). As he raises his arm to block, throw a fast front kick to his stomach.

Illus. 196 (left). You might want to follow the fake with a right roundhouse kick to the head.

The key is to have several options. In addition to combinations and faking techniques, learn to kumite from your left side, your right side, and from the front.

Illus. 197 (right). During a match avoid positioning yourself where one or two of the judges are unable to see your punch or kick. Stay in the middle where you can be seen by all of the judges.

Illus. 198 (left). Avoid turning your back. Try to keep the front of your body in their direct vision. If you are successful with a kick or punch and it is not seen by at least two of the judges, you will get no point.

Illus. 199. There are usually large crowds with much noise at tournaments; so concentrate on your opponent and your fighting skills.

Illus. 200. Your dedication and skill could result in winning the match—maybe the championship.

6
WINNING KATAS

Kata has been called the most important part of karate. In kata, you use planned moves that look like ballet or dance.

Illus. 201. Kata is really the art of karate, and the movements can be beautiful and graceful. Katas also allow you to practise your blocks, kicks, strikes, and punches in a pattern of movements.

Illus. 202 (left). Katas are usually done by one person. You can practise kata alone.

Illus. 203 (above). But kata can also be done in a group.

99

Illus. 204 (right). Judges are looking for good control in your kata. All katas are designed for you to show good form.

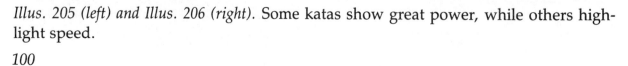

Illus. 205 (left) and Illus. 206 (right). Some katas show great power, while others highlight speed.

Most advanced katas look like movements of an animal such as a cat, a tiger, or a snake. From the ceiling looking downwards katas look like letters of the alphabet, such as H, T, K, or a plus sign (+). Katas have a name, a number, or both. The first kata here is called Heian (*he-on*) One. You follow an H pattern in this kata. The second kata is the "Breathing Dragon" or Seichi (*si-ee-che*). It looks like a dragon breathing deeply as it moves. Form and power are the most important things in these katas.

Illus. 207. Remember, as you approach the judges you will bow, stand, and announce your name and kata. Don't forget to ask for permission to begin your kata.

Illus. 208. After you complete your kata, you will be given a score from one to ten, with ten being the highest. To avoid ties, some tournaments use a decimal system such as 4.2, 3.6, etc.

Heian One

Illus. 209 (right). Stand in a closed stance as you announce your kata. You are facing the judges. Bow.

Illus. 210 (below). Bring up your right leg, cross your arms and breathe in deeply.

Illus. 211 (below, right). Step down into an open stance with fists tightly closed and your arms at your side.

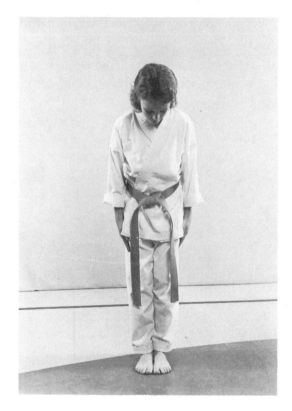

Illus. 212 (left). Move to your left at 90° and do a lower left block in a left front stance.

Illus. 213 (below, left). Step forward into a right front stance as you deliver a right front punch to the chest level.

Illus. 214 (below). Turn 180° to your right and deliver a right downward block.

Illus. 215 (left). Pull your arm in as you sweep-kick with your right foot. Rotate your wrist and swing your fist to your face and circle outward.

Illus. 216 (below, left). Complete the circle with a hammer strike.

Illus. 217 (below). Step up and deliver a left punch to the chest level as you move into a left front stance.

Illus. 218 (right). Turn to face the judges straight ahead. Deliver a low block with the left hand in a left forward stance.

Illus. 219 (far right). Pull your arm inward and shift three-quarters of your weight onto your back leg.

Illus. 220 (below, right). Immediately snap your left arm into an upward rising block. Pretend to grab the arm.

Illus. 221 (bottom right) Step forward and deliver a rising block.

Illus. 222 (right). Step forward and block again with a left rising block. Grab the arm.

Illus. 223 (far right). Step forward into a right stance with a breaking block. Remember to tuck the hand upside down, resting on your hip when it is not blocking or punching.

Illus. 224 (below, right). Turn your body to the far left . . .

Illus. 225 (bottom right). . . . and move into a left lower block in a left front stance.

Illus. 226 (left). Deliver a right front punch in a right front stance.

Illus. 227 (below, left). Begin your turn to the right, and do a right lower block in a right front stance.

Illus. 228 (below). Step up in a left front stance and do a left center punch. *Pay close attention.*

Illus. 229 (right). In the next step, turn to your left and do a left lower block in a left front stance. Your back is now to the judges.

Illus. 230 (below). With the judges behind you, you have just completed a lower left block in a left stance.

Illus. 231 (below, right). Begin to step up with a right punch.

Illus. 232 (left). Complete the punch from a right front stance.

Illus. 233 (below, left). Again prepare to step up and punch with the left hand.

Illus. 234 (below). Complete the punch in a left front stance.

Illus. 235 (above). Prepare to step up and punch with the right hand. Complete the right punch in a right front stance.

Illus. 236 (above, right). Now turn to the left by bringing your right leg far around behind your body.

Illus. 237 (right). Spin into a right back stance and deliver a knife-hand strike with the left hand. You are now facing the judges again.

Illus. 238 (above, left). Step up and place your feet together with your left knife-hand in front and the right hand prepared at your left ear.

Illus. 239 (above). Step out into a 45° angle to the left in a left back stance while striking with a right knife-hand.

Illus. 240 (left). Swing your body to the right and place your left knife-hand in front and draw your right hand, palm inwards, to your left ear.

Illus. 241 (above, right). Deliver a right knife-hand in a left back stance straight ahead.

Illus. 242 (above, far right). Place your left foot close to your right and bring your left hand, palm inward, to your right ear.

Illus. 243 (right). Deliver a left knife strike 45° to the right in a right back stance.

Illus. 244 (far right). Pull your left hand and left foot back and face the judges. Bow.

Breathing Dragon

Illus. 245 (right). Begin the kata with a respectful bow to the judges.

Illus. 246 (below). Raise your leg and arms and breathe out heavily through your mouth.

Illus. 247 (below, right). Pull your right foot into a left cat stance and place open spear hands by your side.

Illus. 248 (above, left). Push out into a horse stance with the right foot in front of the judges.

Illus. 249 (above). Drive spear hands down and breathe heavily outward through your mouth.

Illus. 250 (left). Continue until hands are fully extended.

Illus. 251 (above). Breathe in and pull back your hands, with fists closed.

Illus. 252 (above, right). Continue until your fists are completely behind you.

Illus. 253 (right). Now push your hands outward right in front of your chest and breathe outward. Continue breathing and pushing until your hands are completely extended into a double arm block.

Illus. 254 (left). Breathe in and move into a right cat stance with left foot in front. Place your spear hands at your side.

Illus. 255 (below, left). Turn outward into a full horse stance with left leg in front of the judges.

Illus. 256 (below). Continue until you blow out all air and your hands and arms are fully extended.

Illus. 257 (right). Pull up into a left cat stance with your right foot in front as you breathe in deeply.

Illus. 258 (below). Move outward into a horse stance with right leg facing judges.

Illus. 259 (below, right). Through your mouth, blow out deeply and extend arms into full spear hands.

Illus. 260 (right). Prepare to block in a left crane stance by turning straight towards the judges.

Illus. 261 (below). Step up and rest your left leg behind your right knee off the floor and do a lower block out to your left with your left arm.

Illus. 262 (below, right). Do the same block with your right arm.

Illus. 263 (left). Fall directly back into a right back stance while grabbing the throat with the left hand.

Illus. 264 (below, left). Drive a right elbow strike into the head area. You show this by driving the elbow into your open hand.

Illus. 265 (below). Push the right arm out and choke the neck with the right hand.

Illus. 266 (above). Leave the right hand open and step back into a left back stance.

Illus. 267 (above, right). Drive a left elbow strike into the head. Again, show this by hitting the open hand with the elbow.

Illus. 268 (right). Reach forward with a left choke.

Illus. 269 (left). Drop back again, leaving the left hand out and opened. Drive forward with another elbow strike to the head.

Illus. 270 (below, left). Very gracefully look to the left and prepare a left knife-hand strike.

Illus. 271 (below). Move into a left knife-hand strike in a right cat stance to your left at 90°.

Illus. 272 (left). Pull your right hand back and step up to a left cat stance and deliver a right knife-hand.

Illus. 273 (below, left). Complete the strike at 45° to your right.

Illus. 274 (below). Turn your head and look over your right shoulder.

Illus. 275 (right). Pull your right arm into your left side with your palm open, facing your left cheek. Bring the right leg around. Turn all the way to your left (180° from your first knife strike).

Illus. 276 (below). Move into a left back stance and throw a right knife-hand to the neck.

Illus. 277 (below right). Look 45° to your left. Step forward with your left leg and prepare to move into a right cat stance. Bring your left hand to the right side of your face, palm inward.

Illus. 278 (above). Complete the strike.

Illus. 279 (above, right). Bring your left foot back and move into a closed stance and breathe out.

Illus. 280 (right). Finish with a bow.

Be sure when you are throwing the knife-hand, hold your other hand directly in front of you. For example, with a right knife-hand strike, pull your left hand to the chest.

Illus. 281. This boy performs the Breathing Dragon at a tournament.

Illus. 282. Notice the form and power in his moves.

BEING A WINNER

If you enjoy karate enough and progress well through this book, you will need to find a qualified instructor.

Although an instructor may be excellent for adults, he may not know how to teach you in the best way. You will need more time to learn each karate skill. You cannot master some karate skills because of your age and size. The instructor may not explain things clearly to you like your teacher at school. And he may not have the patience to teach you a new karate skill. The ideal teacher should have an advanced rank in karate (first-degree black belt or higher). He should also have experience as a schoolteacher and a real interest in children. If your karate teacher has these qualities, you will have a better chance for success.

Follow this advice:

1. Find a helpful and patient instructor. Don't get one who screams or hits his students when they make mistakes. You learn from your mistakes—and you're going to make plenty at the beginning. You need someone who won't yell or make you nervous.

2. Take a class with people your own age. You will get confused learning karate with grown-ups. Adults are bigger and their muscles are stronger and better developed than yours. Adult classes move too quickly for young people.

3. Promotion to the next rank should be based on your ability. Although many instructors promote students on their success in a karate tournament, a good instructor should judge you on your ability and not whether or not you win a tournament.

Winning is great, but your confidence will improve when you know you have done your best. Choose an instructor who cares about you and judges your karate ability in class.

Talk with your parents about your interest in karate. Ask them to provide support and guidance. Get their advice when seeking an appropriate instructor. If your parents are able, ask them to study karate with you. Fathers and daughters, mothers and sons, mothers and daughters, and fathers and sons can study together.

Finally, always show respect for the art of karate. Never strike another individual (except in self-defense). Never brag about karate or demonstrate your skills to other boys and girls, or lose your temper and strike out. Always be in control and learn to focus your kicks, punches, and strikes within one inch of the target without hitting. Later on, as you reach levels of brown and black belts, you will have enough control for light contact which will not hurt your opponent.

Read as much as you can about various styles of karate. Karate has different systems and styles, although many are quite similar. Most styles are from Japan, Okinawa, China, and Korea. The style introduced in this book is from Japan and is called Shito-ryu (*shee-toe-ru*). It is most similar to other Japanese styles such as Shotokan (*show-toe-kon*) and Goju-ryu (*go-jew-ru*).

INDEX